BOOM!

DECIPHERING INNOVATION

Named one of
Inc. Magazine's
Top Innovat...

D1637493

*How Disruption Drives Companies to
Transform or Die*

Lisa Hendrickson & Jim Colwick

BOOM!

Deciphering Innovation

How Disruption Drives
Companies to Transform or Die

**Lisa Hendrickson
& Jim Colwick**

TABLE OF CONTENTS

Praise for Boom! Deciphering Innovation: How Disruption Drives Companies to Transform or Die

BOOM! captures the big picture of disruption and innovation. I work with Silicon Valley companies and attend a lot of enterprise tech conferences, and this book sheds light on the current conversations I'm hearing out there. Current business culture is steeped in both the fear of disruption and the veneration of innovation, but there is very little untangling of the economic, technological, and organizational threads that make up these phenomena. Boom! is a quick, evocative read that outlines what's happening and how we got here -- with facts and references! -- and gives business leaders insight into strategies and drivers that can foster innovation within their own organization. While there's no easy pattern for innovation, the themes in this book will stay with you as you and your team weave your futures together.

John Mark Troyer
Co-Founder of TechReckoning and the
Influence Marketing Council

BOOM! picks up where academic books leave off. The hard part of innovation is not the ideas, it's not the disruption or the confusion, it's getting people to change; to let go and leap into the unknown. You have to have good arguments, but reason alone does not suffice. To get people to make these hard decisions requires appealing to both mind and heart, you have to engage the business leaders. That's where this book comes in. The reasons are presented in short, almost pithy, elevator pitches. It provides strong emotional and logical reasons to abandon what's safe and take the leap. I have already found myself quoting this book when appealing to people to step outside of their comfort zone.

Bruce Mackinlay
Director of Innovation and Implementation,
Performant Financial Corporation

The best companies have always found a way to innovate, survive and change to meet the future. In the 21st century where change is coming so quickly that people and institutions are barely able to adapt, it's important for leaders to understand the sources and impact of disruptive change on their organizations. Boom! is a good first step in learning about today's business landscape and the key questions leaders must answer to prepare themselves and their organizations to excel in this digital world. It is a quick, interesting, and provocative read. I recommend it.

Doug Dichting
President, Meadowview Enterprises LLC; Former VP of Research and Innovation for Del Monte Foods; and Group Director, Global R&D for The Coca Cola Company

"IN THE LONG HISTORY OF HUMANKIND (AND ANIMAL KIND, TOO) THOSE WHO LEARNED TO COLLABORATE AND IMPROVISE MOST EFFECTIVELY HAVE PREVAILED."

Charles Darwin
On The Origin of Species, 1859

WINNING IN AN AGE OF RELENTLESS CHANGE AND DISRUPTION

You know you should be innovating or your business will be in trouble soon.

You're having a hard time getting started. You're so busy trying to keep the current business going.

What do they mean by innovation anyway?
We know. We've been through this. We didn't know how to innovate either. **Until we did.**

Dear Industry Leader,

We've written this 30,000 foot guide for leaders like you who see the disruptive writing on the wall. You've told us you want a simple to comprehend text to understand the global forces driving the massive changes that are transforming your market right before your eyes (and you're feeling it on your balance sheet).

You've already heard the BOOM! in your market and felt the disruption. Inaction breeds dislocation and before you know it, your customer is someone else's. How do you innovate?

We're giving you a quick way of getting a handle on innovation and disruption without all of the lingo and jargon, so that it stops being a buzzy thing your marketing people are telling you about and becomes something tangible that you can see as your next best step to what's next.

You can start engaging with these global forces before it's too late to make up for the lost ground of inertia. We're here to help your company transform into a digital organization that only now you are imagining.

You may not find people in your organization willing to tell you the skinny, but we will. Think of us as your trusted advisors, who are willing to pull the band-aid off fast and know how to remedy the situation so that you're good to go.

Leaders approach change in one of two ways: excited or running scared. We want you to be excited about the possibilities of the future.

We're with you on this.

Lisa Hendrickson & Jim Colwick

WHAT HAPPENED?

Toto, we're not in Kansas anymore.

Every day there's more news about how businesses are being upset and the fabric of companies is becoming unglued.

"How did Uber devise a revolutionary taxi service without owning a single vehicle? Netflix is the largest movie theater on the planet—how were they able to develop a plan to achieve that without owning even one movie house? . . . Why didn't massive hospitality companies such as Marriott and Hilton come up with the billion-dollar concept used by Airbnb?"

Daniel Burris
The Anticipatory Organization[1]

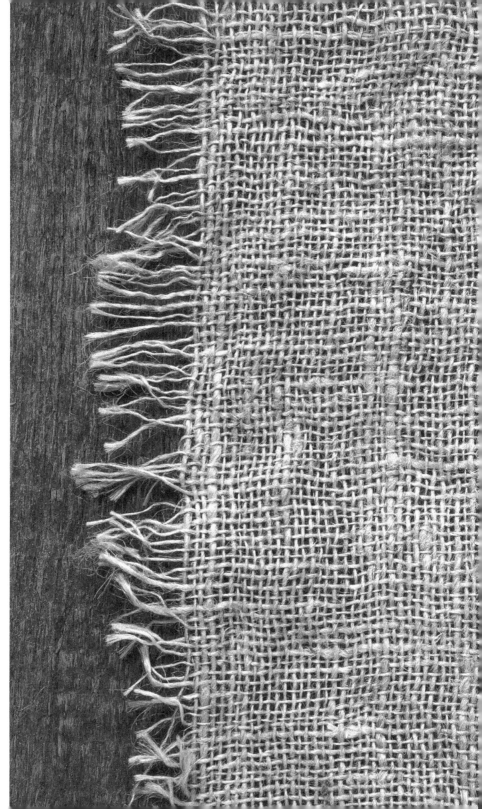

Disruption used to mean a telemarketer calling at suppertime. Not so much anymore.

Sometimes we confuse disruption with interruption. It's bothersome to be interrupted, but then you'd just get back to what you were doing. Not anymore. This is different and it's serious.

Imagine spending all that money laying millions of miles of telephone lines and then having your customers just use their cellphones. That's disruption.

What Happened?

What happened?

This happened.

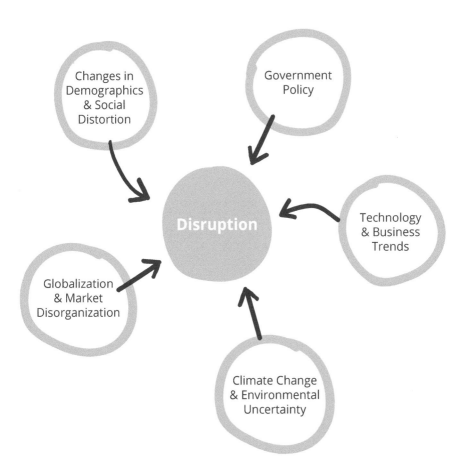

Disruptive change is coming from many directions.

Q: When China sneezes does your sales team catch a cold?

A: Used to be this question seemed silly, but now you have to stop and consider the answer.

Globalization and Market Disorganization

Brexit! Who would have "thunk it"? Where have all the jobs gone?

Government Policy

Government innovation and regulation can accelerate or inhibit markets. Remember who invented the Internet? The U.S. government did. China's policies on market entry make possible or defeat companies from entering their markets. And this is just a starter list.

Climate Change & Environmental Uncertainty

Hurricanes in NYC? Huh? Hurricane Sandy...remember that? The Jersey Shore does. And now it's Irma and Harvey making their acquaintance with Florida and Texas, respectively.

Technology and Business Trends

"Software is eating the world." Marc Andreesen

It used to be that you knew all the cool new companies and then ate them for breakfast. Now they're eating your lunch.

Changes in Demographics and Social Distortion

Shifting populations and world conflicts are changing expectations and needs that can impact your society, your company and you personally. Examples include: generational differences, wars, political instability, mass migrations, and culture clashes.

THE DISRUPTED LANDSCAPE

Take notice and recognize the difference.

DISRUPTION

"Disruption is what happens when someone does something clever that makes you or your company look obsolete."

DISLOCATION

"Dislocation is when the whole environment is being altered so quickly that everyone starts to feel they can't keep up...that our societal structures are failing to keep pace with the rate of change."

Craig Mundie,
Former Chief of Strategy and Research at Microsoft[2]

Be prepared or be gone.

It's not whether getting on the "innovation bandwagon" is good or bad...we're not navel gazers contemplating if the ancients ate tuna salad or arguing for a best practice.

We're telling you that winter is coming and you've got to get your strategy together so that you all come out alive and well to see the flowers in the spring.

These mega forces are converging in a loud BOOM!

IoT = Internet of Things

AI = Artificial Intelligence

AR = Augmented Reality

Big Data

Blockchain

VR = Virtual Reality

SM = Social Media

What's next?

31

Digital transformation is everywhere.

How does digital transformation impact you?

What happens when companies are caught off guard?

Traditional businesses are upended by upstarts in the marketplace penetrating and changing markets in better ways for consumers.

People won't go back doing it the old way. People aren't going to give up their Smartphones for a "Dumbphone."

Battles lost to innovation and industry disruption.

Smart phone innovation crushed Blackberry's success. Its stock dropped almost

95% from 2008 to 2015.[3]

2008   2015

Internet advertising bludgeoned the print industry. **From 1950 to 2005, print revenues grew from roughly $20 billion to $60 billion.**

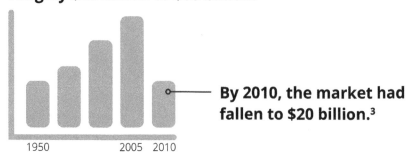

By 2010, the market had fallen to $20 billion.[3]

1950   2005   2010

THE DISRUPTED LANDSCAPE

How does it feel?

How do you know when it's happening to you?

Take a look at some typical warning signals.

Your brand slips.

Your brand isn't sexy anymore, not because you've gotten some shade on Twitter, but you know it's coming.

You're losing your customers to other newer, cooler brands that have a different relationship with their customers (who used to be your customers).

THE DISRUPTED LANDSCAPE

Investors don't love you anymore.

It used to be that you couldn't wait for quarterly reports because you could see your stock options flourishing.

Now there are lots of venture and investment dollars flooding the market, but you're not getting any investor love.

Upstarts are everywhere.

Small companies are eating away at the edges of your marketplace at an alarming rate.

It's like having ants at your company picnic and they've ruined the potato salad. Next, they're headed for the burgers.

And, new business models are changing the marketplace.

It feels like a fashion fad to you, except now you're the one who looks like an old fogey.

That's OK, you're tough and you can tough it out...except now you actually are trying to play catch up.

Question is, can you catch up?

B

C

D

E

H

J

K

Your model has blown up and you can't go back.

Disintermediation used to mean that you saved money in operations. Now you walk the floor of your company, and it's filled with temps that you don't know.

Are these people the ones that really know what your customers want now?

Discounting has become your primary sales strategy.

Conversations at your weekly finance meetings used to start with reviewing top line revenue. Now it's all about holding onto those margin gains.

Salespeople are complaining that selling to Dick, "the King of Couponing", is a drag because he has all the leverage.

Employees are asking, "Does the emperor have clothes?"

Your customers are changing, but you're not.

Your customers have left you but you don't know it.

It's like a girlfriend that's planning to send you a breakup text, but she's been too busy with her new boyfriend.

Loyalty means different things to different people.

Customer loyalty isn't like it was...

It's different now... customers want transparency, sustainability, social purpose, instant shipping, and inexpensive organic goods. And, they want to feel like you're paying extra special attention to them. Plus, having the right Google ranking makes all the difference in the world.

The rise of customer empowerment means that your customers might not need you in the very near future.

BLOOD AND TREASURE. THE BONEYARD OF THE GREATS

What happened to all the Blood and Treasure—the strategy, hard work, investments, and accomplishments? And now it is lost. Only the skeleton is left.

Even the Disruptors are being disrupted.

"A disruptive change hits a market, making what used to be complicated simple and what used to be expensive affordable. Lumbering giants move too slowly, toppling under their own weight...Then enterprising upstarts become lumbering giants, destined to be felled by the next generation of entrepreneurs."

Scott D. Anthony, Clark G. Gilbert, and Mark W. Johnson
Dual Transformation[3]

Fortune 500 firms in 1955 vs. 2014;

88% are gone

and we're all better off because of that dynamic creative destruction.[4]

Detroit Steel

Armstrong Rubber

Zenith Electronics Cone Mills Brown Shoe

Pacific Vegetable Oil Collins Radio

Studebaker National Sugar Refining

American Motors

Hines Lumber

Riegel Textiles

Buying old tech ≠ innovation.

In 2007, Nokia was the market leader in mobile with 3x the market share of its nearest competitor.

● ● ●

Also in 2007, two industry disruptions made a big BOOM into the market: the iPhone and Android operating system came to market.

● ● ●

Over the next 6 years, Nokia saw its market demolished by smartphone innovation.

● ● ●

In 2013, Nokia sold its handset business to Microsoft.

● ● ●

Eighteen months later, Microsoft took a $7.6 billion write-down on that acquisition.

● ● ●

Microsoft tried to find a leadership position with a back-of-the-pack acquisition.[3]

Let the market help you determine the market. Minimally viable product (MVP) replaces traditional R&D.

Kodak (f. 1888), for decades was the world leader in photography. Heavy investments in digital imaging in the 90's might have made a new product market but its people didn't understand its own digital landscape.

. . .

On top of that, cut rate market disruptors from Japan changed the value proposition for film. Kodak didn't answer the call.

. . .

Kodak filed for Chapter 11 bankruptcy protection in 2012.[3]

. . .

Innovating a product that disrupts a market, when you're not disrupting yourself at the same time, doesn't give your company an advantage in a market that you've made.

A new technology can radically change an entire industry.

When Amazon introduced eCommerce to disrupt the book industry, over 4,000 independent and big box bookstores bit the dust.[5]

Next Up: Amazon went after retailers.

In 2006, brick and mortar retail was hot. The collective market caps of Walmart, Target, Best Buy, Nordstrom, Kohl's, J. C. Penney, Sears, and Macy's retailers were worth $400 billion, and Amazon was only valued at $17.5 billion.

In 2016, it was estimated that the revenues of these market leaders was equal to just 62% of their totals in 2006.[5]

That same technology can leave a path of scorched earth.

Store closures will push
30% of U.S. malls
to the brink of closing.

Hundreds of U. S. shopping
malls are at risk.[6]

"Since the start of the year (2017), more than 1,500 store closures have been announced by major retailers with most of closures happening within the year."[6]

Playing Catch Up?

You invested bigly on your current model, but it's just not producing what you need to make all the players happy.

You think "that's OK, we're tough and we can tough it out…" except deep down you know you're actually trying to play catch up.

Question is, can you catch up?

If you think the disruption bus isn't coming for you, it just hasn't reached your stop.

The hard won success of your business is too much to lose. No industry will be left untouched.

Appliances / Durable Goods

Automobiles

Consulting

Government

Grocery

Education

Energy

Entertainment

Financial Services

Furnishings

Hospitality

Healthcare

Manufacturing

Online Companies

Retail

Software

Transportation

...to name just a few

Is What You're Doing Working?

The question isn't whether you should innovate. The question is, do you need a new business model?

You don't want to be the one swept away when you had another path away from the storm that would have taken you to new opportunities.

The storm is coming and it's coming for you. Duck and cover won't work for your current business model. It just won't.

PURE INNOVATION.
WHAT'S THE FORMULA?

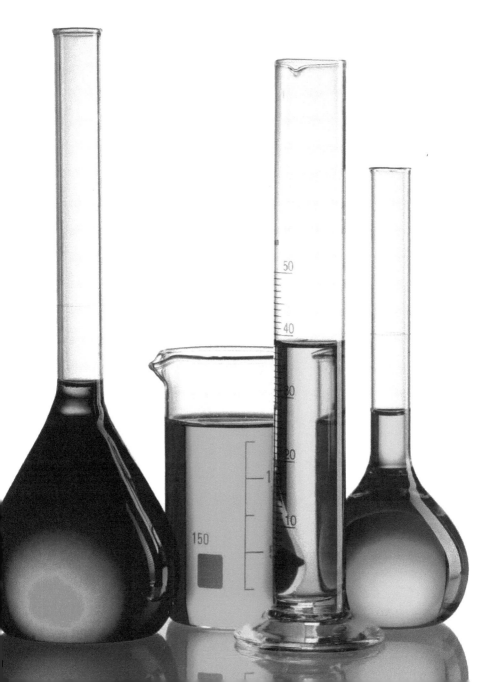

What is innovation?

"Innovation is the act of discovering new opportunities by looking beyond commonly held views, by questioning rather than accepting the limitations that conventional wisdom imposes."

Langdon Morris, Moses MA, and Po Chi Wu.
Agile Innovation[7]

Pure innovation.
What's the formula?

Different Ways Companies Can Innovate

WHO	WHAT	WHERE	HOW
Customers	**Offerings**	**Presence**	**Process**
Customer experience	Platforms	Brand	Process innovation
	Solutions	Networking	
Value capture			Organizational structure

Adapted from the classic article "12 Different Ways for Companies to Innovate." *MIT Sloan Management Review*, Spring 2006, by Mohanbir Sawhney, Robert C. Wolcott and Inigo Arroniz[8]

Different Ways Companies Can Innovate

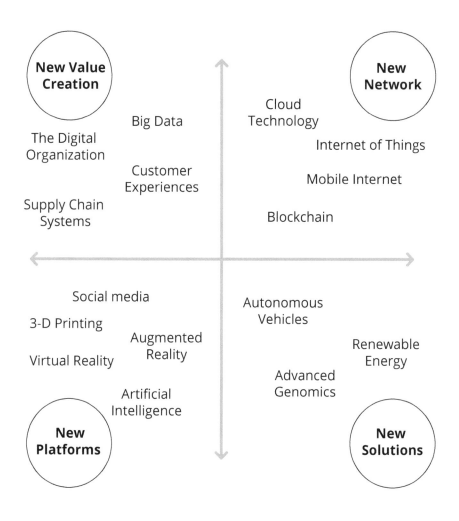

New Value Creation

Big Data

Cloud Technology

New Network

The Digital Organization

Internet of Things

Customer Experiences

Mobile Internet

Supply Chain Systems

Blockchain

Social media

Autonomous Vehicles

3-D Printing

Augmented Reality

Renewable Energy

Virtual Reality

Advanced Genomics

Artificial Intelligence

New Platforms

New Solutions

PURE INNOVATION

Netflix won by disrupting itself.

First Netflix disrupted Blockbuster's store-based film rental model, by mailing out rented DVDs to customers.

Then Netflix disrupted itself. By abandoning mailing as a main strategy to embracing the future which is / was downloading, Netflix refined its downloading game.

Then, Netflix moved into the original content game, competing now with movie theaters.

See how all that played out?
Now they're a FANG* and in the cool kids club.

● ● ●

Pure innovation.

*Facebook, Amazon, Netflix, Google

PURE INNOVATION

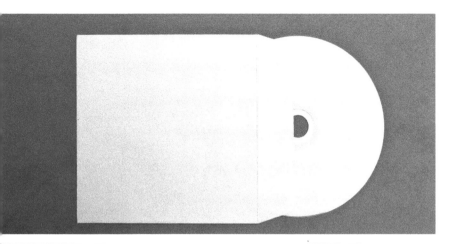

Wheels turning?

How can you take your current business and transition it through a new technology platform so that you can increase your offerings and your customer base?

We challenge you, and your team, to create something unique. Something that will move your company from a super-crowded field, who are all playing a race to the bottom, to a wide-open first mover advantage game driven by you.

That's right.

TRANSITING?

Moving doesn't mean orderly, known and expected.

In fact, it's kind of messy.

We're Between Things.

We're in transit from the industrial economy, next stop the New, New Economy.

"Simply put, only organizations that innovate have a chance of survival in the long run. Those that don't...will not."

Langdon Morris, Moses MA, and Po Chi Wu.
Agile Innovation7

**New World of
Opportunities and Upsets**

There is a confluence of forces transforming every aspect of modern life.

It's not your fault. It's like when Lehman Brothers was leveraged 35:1 and you lost your job.

It really isn't about you personally, but you do have to do something, so that you're able to compete and thrive in the new world.

Transformation means to make anew.

Don't think rehashing products or firing your marketing department is transforming your company.

Nokia started out as a rubber boot company. Then it became a mobile phone company. Next it sold itself to Microsoft. Now it's a communications and information company.

Marriott moved from a root beer stand to a worldwide hotel chain.[3]

Dislocation doesn't mean disenfranchised.

When we transform a company, there is the loss of the previous. The previous we loved because we were the center of the universe. The previous where the sun shined on our company in the form of accolades.

Backslapping is replaced now with glad handing, and we don't know where we'll end up. All we know is that what used to be isn't there anymore. We're sad about this.

* * *

Market dislocation doesn't mean you don't have the power to make a move and make a new market.

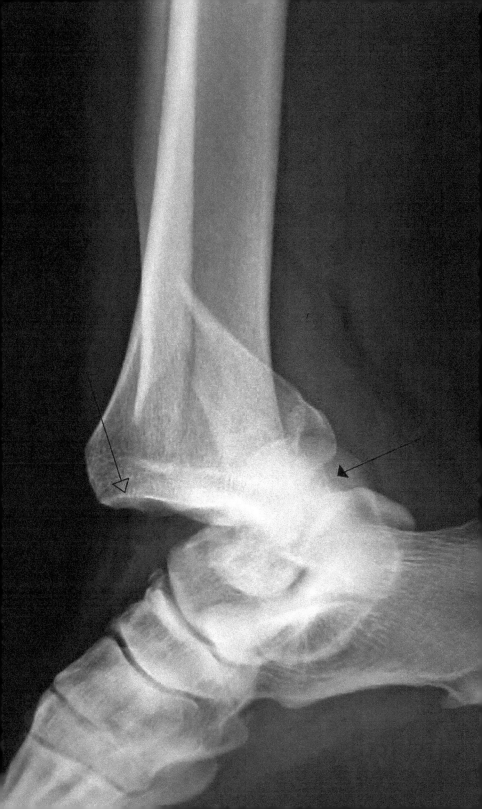

Changing the game at the bottom of the 9th.

Changing is difficult and most of us only do when its too painful to stay the course. We don't want to wait to change at the bottom of the 9th, because unless it's a very special game, the outcome is already determined.

Happiness comes from problem solving. Not from avoiding the problem.

It only feels like lack when we think we're not going to get anything else.

• • •

All opportunity lives in uncertainty. If you knew how the story would end, you wouldn't read the book.

Chimera, it's a mythical creature and your company will resemble it shortly.

The Chimera is a mythical creature that is the integration of a lion, a goat and a snake.

Like the Chimera, your company will have a few different natures, some at odds with itself.

Know that you won't be going back to doing or being just one thing.

In disruption, companies may have to be in more than one mode of operating to serve the market's rapidly changing expectations.

TRANSITING

Overwhelming? Maybe. Achievable outcome? Yes.

You can do this. You really can. We've told you about others who have and done so successfully.

You can do this.

YOUR INNOVATION STRATEGY

Moving from Market Disruption to Innovation

Look at innovation as an intersection.

Innovation occurs when the fringe of one vertical or industry comes in contact with the fringe of another.

With just a small amount of overlap, innovation can occur as people, technology, process, product, or market features can be borrowed and made anew inside another vertical (with no intention of returning what was borrowed).

INNOVATION STRATEGY

There are no sacred cows.

Your Business Model

Your next business model is the startup that will eat your lunch and your market.

Maybe the best defense against the next disruptive startup looking to take your market, is for you to cannibalize your current business so that you can keep and then grow market share.

Sounds radical?

Remember, Netflix cannibalized its own DVD business for its downloading business.

Disrupt your company's strategy, invent a new future.

It was simpler when you were either a leader or a follower.

Now this doesn't even describe the turbulence in your market.

The definition of market leadership has changed. The stakes are higher.

Leadership is innovating so that your company renews its product and services in a way that serves the next economy.

Rigidity is out. Strategic agility is in.

Ever been to a sandwich shop where you've got to order off of a menu that's numbered? "Give me a number 6 please" and before you know it you've got a sandwich. And oh yeah, no substitutions—it says so right on the menu.

Now it's mass customization and everyone gets to have what they want when they want it.

The only hard and fast rule now is not thinking that you've got hard and fast rules.

From strategic agility will come a new product or service line and a way new of doing business.

ACON & TOMATO	5.25
D SWISS	4.00
R HAM	5.00
	4.50
& TOMATO	4.95
HERO/ROLL	5.95
ANDWICH	6.95

Cement shoes no more.

Architecture is newly flexible inside the organization, its technology and real estate footprint.

Long term real estate contracts brought down a fair number of dot coms from the boom and bust years of Web 1.0.

This round of innovation includes flexible workspaces and flexible workers. Workforces expand and contract with new business requirements.

Get ready to change your web architecture to accommodate new remote employees and technical norms. It's easier to use #Slack* to message your team than it is to get in a room all together.

No need to build this architecture like the Pyramids. It won't last for 1000 years (and it won't have to).

*#Slack is a platform that connects teams with the apps, services, and resources they need to get work done. www.Slack.com

Cultures are Enculturating.

Few axioms from the industrial age fit with today's market disruption. This one, however, is for the ages.

"Culture eats strategy for breakfast." Peter Drucker.

If there's anything that you want to nurture, it's your company's culture.

The quandary now is how do you build a culture when you have contractors, temporary employees, and a flexible workforce?

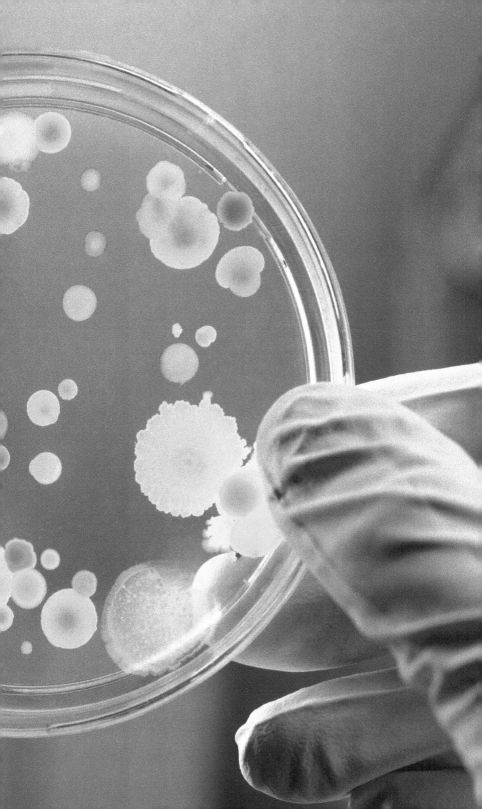

People still need to grow.

No matter how innovative your software, products, and services are, you still have the human element to contend with. This means that people interpret situations and service through different lenses.

No matter how great the tool, it's people who will sell it and break down the barriers between the technology and the humans it's supposed to help.

In a rapidly changing environment, coaching and training for your employees and contractors are needed more than ever.

Training is what everyone will need to follow your lead.

Getting to work now that you've arrived.

All of this talk about innovation is intellectually challenging and for some of us, it's even fun. Then there is moving from the conversation of strategy to the work of execution.

Who's on your team? What thinking tools of innovation do they have in their tool belt? Can they deliver on the promise of your brand and company?

The proof is in what you do everyday.

COACHING

How to Foster Innovation

Don't be afraid to let go of your mess.

We all make messes. Don't be afraid to let go of messes from the past and the messes that you'll make in trying to figure out the future.

Messes don't look very nice and they might smell bad. Knowing when you need to let go of what is weighing you down (old ways of thinking, sunk costs, fear of change, to name a few) is a gift.

Don't be a Slave to the Corporate Past...

Corporate slavery has it own language. It sounds like:

We just don't do it this way.

We tried that and it didn't work.

Corporate won't let us do that.

We don't have the time or resources.

We have managers for that.

Let's put that on the parking lot.

I've been here a lot longer than you have. Once you're here as long as I've been, then you'll have a chance to leave your mark.

Disrupt yourself.

According to Gallup's 2017 *State of the American Workplace* report,

70%
of U.S. workers are not engaged at work—"they're just there."

Worldwide, 87%
of employees are not engaged.[9]

What part of Workforce Engagement do you not understand? Better engagement is where you'll see the most gain.

Ready to start putting your toe in the water? Begin by answering these questions:

How can you take your current business (seeing this as a starting point) and transition it through technology so that you can increase your customer base and operational performance?

> And then create something unique so you move from a super-crowded field of competitors to a wide *Blue Ocean Strategy*[10].

Given your current competitive environment, how important is it to create more innovative products and services? How much time do you have to get this done?

What is your current organizational capability to create or enhance innovation (e.g., leadership, people proficient in innovation technology, structure to support innovation, culture)?

> What do you need to change? Where do you need help?

What will you personally own and who will you ask to take on innovation leadership?

What are your biggest obstacles to innovation in your organization?

OK, we think you can take it from here.

We think you've got some good training wheels on now, and we've got one more piece of advice for you:

You're learning something new. Be kind to yourself and others in the process.

When you were a child you didn't fail to ride the bike when you fell down, you were learning to ride the bike. Remember how that went—at first you didn't know how to ride a bike and then all of a sudden you did.

Even if you haven't ridden a bike in many years, you know you can still hop of a bike and ride any time you want. That's because you learned something intrinsic about balance and once you know that, you'll never unlearn it.

Now, go off and ride.

Dear Industry Leader,

We've given you the straight talk about innovation and disruption. We hope you can see the possibilities of transforming your company by innovating across your products, services, people and organization.

Disruption is scary. Innovation is exciting. Maybe just acknowledging the market disruption will move the challenge from scary to exciting for you. We hope so, because we think that innovation is a great journey—one that starts with the spark of inspiration.

If someone would offer us a carrot or a stick, we'd both pick the carrot. It tastes better and overall, we like the concept. We think if you choose to innovate, you're choosing the carrot. There's always the stick but really, what kind of fun is that?

We hope our book has helped you understand how market disruption relates to innovation, and how innovation can impact the market and your organization. Need more from us? We've got some great resources in the End Notes for you, plus we're sharing our coordinates so wherever you are in the innovation universe, you can reach us.

We're with you on this.

Lisa Hendrickson & Jim Colwick

Lisa Hendrickson

Lisa Hendrickson sold her first idea for a company to her father when she was five years old for twenty-five cents. Today she is a serial entrepreneur who has lived an immersive life around start-up ventures. She is the founder of Spark City, a "Thinking Partner" consultancy that helps companies trail blaze new products, services and business models. Prior, she was the COO of HCC, an award-winning pioneering sustainable luxury interiors company that became one of the fastest growing inner city companies in America garnering a coveted slot in the ICIC 100. She's been a featured speaker at both Inc 500 and Inc Magazine's GrowCo conferences.

She is the creator of many entrepreneurial programs including the FutureLAB series, Audacity, Morning Salon, and The Sustainable Organization. She is an Adjunct Professor of Business at FIT teaching Entrepreneurship and Sustainability where she is also the program designer for "Finance for Design." She has appeared in The New York Times, BBC World Business Report, CBS's The Early Show, ABC's World News Tonight, Crain's NY, and many other fine news outlets.

Jim Colwick

For over 25 years, Jim Colwick has worked with executive teams to reshape their futures, ranging from initiatives to improve corporate performance to the design and implementation of new business models taking advantage of disruptions in the marketplace. Jim specializes in executive alignment, accelerated strategy, workforce engagement, and development of agile organizations.

His clients have included Fortune 500, mid-size and entrepreneurial corporations in advanced technology, energy, financial services, healthcare, manufacturing, transportation, and government. Jim has also held senior leadership positions in innovative, high-growth, technology consultancies focused on business strategy, technology optimization, customer experience and business transformation.

Want more?

Here's more.

Get in touch:

lhendrickson@sparkcity.co
jim.colwick@integralchange.com

@lisamax
@jcolwick

linkedin.com/in/lisahendrickson
linkedin.com/in/jimcolwick

More from us:

The New Physicality of Customer Experience: Web Customer Centricity Overflowing into Real Spaces by Lisa Hendrickson

The Sh*FT Method: Innovating from the Inside Out, a web training series, www.facebook.com/sparkcityglobal

End notes:

1. Daniel Burris, The Anticipatory Organization: Turn Disruption and Change into Opportunity and Advantage (Austin, TX: Greenleaf Book Group Press, 2017)

2. Thomas L. Friedman, Thank You For Being Late: An Optimist's Guide to Thriving In the Age of Accelerations, pp. 27-29 (New York: Farrar, Straus and Giroux, 2016)

3. Scott D. Anthony, Clark G. Gilbert, and Mark W. Johnson, Dual Transformation: How to Position Today's Business While Creating the Future (Boston: Harvard Business School Press, 2017)

4. Professor Mark J. Perry's AEI Blog. http://www.aei.org/publication/fortune-500-firms-in-1955-vs-2014-89-are-gone-and-were-all-better-off-because-of-that-dynamic-creative-destruction/

5. Visual Capitalist, December 30, 2016

6. Business Insider, March 7, 2017

7. Langdon Morris, Moses MA, and Po Chi Wu. Agile Innovation (Hoboken, NJ: John Wiley & Sons, Inc., 2014)

8. Mohanbir Sawhney, Robert C. Wolcott, and Inigo Arroniz. "12 Different Ways for Companies to Innovate", MIT Sloan Management Review, Spring 2006.

9. Gallup State of the American Workplace, February 2017

10. W. Chan Kin and Rewnee Mauborgne. *Blue Ocean Strategy: How to Create Uncontested Market Space and Make the Competition Irrelevant.* (Boston: Harvard Business Press, 2005).

Photo credits:

Page 1: Design by Olivia Greco

Page 4: iStock vm

Page 7: Shutterstock Pavel L Photo and Video

Page 8: Shutterstock Serge Ka

Page 9: iStock 157510961 photo credit catscan.com

Page 10: Illustration by Olivia Greco

Page 13: iStock Sue Felderg 466395505

Page 14: find a watermark—doctored by Olivia Greco

Page 15: iStock BraunS

Page 16: Veer stock photo

Page 17: iStock Sykono

Page 18: iStock Dragon Images

Page 19: Reuters photo credit Eduard Munoz/ Reuters 2007

Page 20: Veer 8948546

Page 21: Veer

Page 22: 1958 Spring/Summer Sears Catalogue

Page 23: Veer

Page 24: The Car Connection http://www.thecarconnection.com/

Page 25: Veer

Page 26: Shutterstock surekin_son

Page 27: http://www.aviationexplorer.com/updated_airliner_boneyard_photos/images/Boneyard_18_jpg.jpg

Page 29: https://www.retailnews.asia/wp-content/uploads/2016/01/china-stock.jpg

Page 30: iStock photo Credit Owen Price

Page 31: WROC Rochester, July 19, 2015 from video

Page 32: iStock Alan P

Page 33: iStock Version Photography

Page 34: The Daily Mail, AFP/Getty Images

Page 35: By Frank Hank - Own work, CC BY-SA 3.0, https://commons.wikimedia.org/w/index.php?curid=31466645